Did Yo

SOUTH Y

A MISCELLA₁

Compiled by Julia Skinner

With particular reference to the work of Clive Hardy,
Melvyn Jones and Roly Smith

THE FRANCIS FRITH COLLECTION

www.francisfrith.com

First published in the United Kingdom in 2011 by The Francis Frith Collection®

This edition published exclusively for Bradwell Books in 2013
For trade enquiries see: www.bradwellbooks.com or tel: 0800 834 920
ISBN 978-1-84589-536-5

British Library Cataloguing in Publication Data

Did You Know? South Yorkshire - A Miscellany
Compiled by Julia Skinner
With particular reference to the work of Clive Hardy, Melvyn Jones and Roly Smith

The Francis Frith Collection
6 Oakley Business Park,
Wylye Road, Dinton,
Wiltshire SP3 5EU
Tel: +44 (0) 1722 716 376
Email: info@francisfrith.co.uk
www.francisfrith.com

Printed and bound in Malaysia
Contains material sourced from responsibly managed forests

Front Cover: **DONCASTER, STATION ROAD 1903** 49854p
Frontispiece: **ROTHERHAM, THE TOWN CENTRE c1965** R60043

The colour-tinting is for illustrative purposes only, and is not intended to be historically accurate

CONTENTS

INTRODUCTION

In 1974 the Local Government Act of 1972 came into effect which saw the abolition of the historic three Ridings administrative areas of Yorkshire. It was the Viking Danes who first divided the huge county of Yorkshire into the ridings, or 'thridings' (thirds), but under the provisions of the Act their place was taken by three new metropolitan counties of West, North and South Yorkshire. When South Yorkshire came into being in 1974 it was still an industrial powerhouse founded on coal, steelmaking and heavy industry centred on Sheffield, Rotherham, Doncaster and Barnsley.

Sheffield has been famous since the 14th century for cutlery, but it was the discovery in the 18th century that steel could be purified by using a crucible that led to Sheffield becoming the steel capital of Britain. Forges, metal-working shops and steelworks came in all shapes and sizes, from those employing just a handful of men to the industrial giants like Firth Brown and Hadfields. There were other industries, such as the Yorkshire Engine Co, which built railway locomotives, and there were also several collieries within easy reach of the city centre. Sheffield was badly damaged by enemy bombing in the Second World War, and following the wartime devastation much of the city centre was rebuilt; little now survives of the pre-Victorian era save for parts of the cathedral and a handful of houses. Sheffield is still a steelmaking area, but this industry no longer provides employment on a massive scale.

Coal mining was of great importance to the development and economy not only of the major towns of the region like Barnsley, Doncaster and Rotherham (which also had an important iron and steel making industry) but also many smaller villages in the South Yorkshire coalfield in the 19th and 20th centuries; but coal miners paid the price for taking on the Thatcher Government in 1984, and after a strike lasting just under a year the miners were back at work with nothing to show for their stand. Retribution came in the form of closures, including profitable or potentially profitable pits; and as the remaining collieries were privatised, the NCB ceased to exist.

The popular perception of South Yorkshire is that it is an industrial landscape, but between the great industrial centres are some delightful old manorial villages. Just out of Sheffield on the way into Derbyshire are some charming little places, and within the Barnsley and Doncaster areas there are many quiet rural hamlets that have a history going back over a thousand years. The wealth that South Yorkshire's industry created for the local landowners is also on show in the magnificent houses that they built in the region, such as Wentworth Woodhouse, four miles north-west of Rotherham (see photograph W233006, below), which is one of England's forgotten treasures. This great 18th-century Palladian mansion has a 600-foot frontage, one of the longest in England; it was built by Thomas Watson-Wentworth, 1st Marquess of Rockingham (1693-1750) and extended by his heir, and became the home of the Fitzwilliam family in the 19th century. It is now privately owned.

WENTWORTH WOODHOUSE c1965 W233006

SOUTH YORKSHIRE DIALECT WORDS AND PHRASES

'Well, I'll go to the foot o' our stairs!'- I'm really surprised!

'Clemmed' - very cold, frozen through.

'Nesh' - feeling the cold, as in 'I'm a bit nesh'.

'Jennel' - a name used in Sheffield for the covered passage that linked back-to-back houses facing the street with those in the courtyard behind.

'Laikin' - skiving off school or work.

'Mardy' - peevish, querulous, miserable, moody, sulking.

'Snicket' - a pathway, between hedges, fences etc.

'I'm stood 'ere like Clem Alice!' - I'm standing here waiting, looking like a complete idiot!

'It's a bit black over Bill's mother's'- It looks like it might rain.

The Yorkshire version of the 'See No Evil, Hear No Evil' saying:
See al
Hear all
Say nowt

Eyt all
Sup all
Pay nowt

An' if tha does owt for nowt,
Do it for thissen.

SHEFFIELD, THE STEEL
GIANT SCULPTURE
BOWDEN HOUSTEADS
WOOD 2005 S108710

HAUNTED SOUTH YORKSHIRE

One of Sheffield's most famous ghost stories is that the shade of Mary, Queen of Scots is reputed to haunt the Turret House of Sheffield Manor Lodge, where the tragic queen spent part of her long period of captivity in the reign of Elizabeth I before her eventual execution for plotting to take Elizabeth's throne. There have been several reported sightings of a beautiful lady dressed in black who glides across the floor and disappears through walls, and a ghostly face is said to sometimes look out from a window of the Turret House.

The title of Sheffield's most haunted pub is claimed by Carbrook Hall at Attercliffe Common. Psychic investigations have identified one of the ghosts as Colonel John Bright, a Parliamentarian soldier from the time of the Civil War, although he is said to be a peaceful, benevolent spirit. Colonel Bright was a real person who lived in the Hall before it became a pub, and rode to York to ask for artillery support during the war, when Sheffield Castle was about to be taken by Royalist forces. Amongst a number of other ghosts alleged to haunt the pub are an elderly woman, a monk, and another Parliamentarian soldier from the Civil War period. A mysterious shadowy entity is also said to haunt the bar, sometimes throwing items around.

The main road at Hickleton near Doncaster is said to be haunted by a phantom highwayman, who sometimes appears headless, and sometimes wearing a tricorn hat. Hickleton is famous for three skulls which are displayed in a glass case in the lychgate of the parish church, accompanied by a warning of mortality: 'Today for me, tomorrow for thee'. One theory is that they are the skulls of executed highwayman, and perhaps it is the spirit of one of them that haunts the road.

The historic building which currently houses the Cromwell's Restaurant in Church Street in Conisbrough, near Doncaster, is said to be haunted by a figure wearing a long cloak and a feathered hat which has been seen rushing up the stairs before disappearing. Other strange phenomena have been noted, such as doors being mysteriously slammed shut and unexplained sudden drops in temperature. The ghost of a man who appears to be dressed in the garb of a farm labourer of the past has also been seen there. A spectral grey monk is also said to haunt the nearby ruins of Conisbrough Castle.

Several strange events were reported when the Stocksbridge Bypass on the A616 north west of Sheffield was being built in the 1980s. Many workmen said that they had seen a group of mysterious children dressed in old-fashioned clothes on the site at night, singing, dancing and playing, but there were no traces of their footsteps in the muddy ground the next day. Another strange apparition that is supposed to haunt the area of the bypass is that of a monk, and a clairvoyant has claimed that the contractors who built the road disturbed the monk's grave during its construction. In recent years the bypass has been claimed to be the second most haunted road in Britain by the Paranormal Research Foundation.

The Red Rum pub at Cemetery Road in Grimethorpe, Barnsley, is reputedly haunted by the ghost of a woman wearing a long skirt and a cap, who has been seen walking through the bar before suddenly disappearing, and who seems to open doors for people to pass through. She has been seen regularly by both customers and staff, and is believed to the shade of a woman who died in the building in the 19th century.

The Bluecoat pub at The Crofts in Rotherham is said to be haunted by the sound of a crying child. Another haunted pub in the town is The Earl of Stafford at Hooton Roberts, which is reputedly haunted by the ghost of a young woman who hanged herself from the banister of the stairs after her father forbade her to see her lover, a local baker's son.

SOUTH YORKSHIRE MISCELLANY

Following the Norman Conquest of 1066, the conquerors established a town at Sheffield immediately to the south-west of the confluence of the Rivers Don and Sheaf. The first castle at Sheffield dates from the 12th century when William de Lovetot built a motte and bailey castle. The two rivers formed a natural moat to the castle on the north and east. This castle was replaced with a stone structure in the second half of the 13th century. During the Civil War the castle at Sheffield was garrisoned for the king, but was surrendered to Parliament in 1644. The castle was largely demolished on Cromwell's orders in the late 1640s, after which it was plundered for building stone by local people.

SHEFFIELD, FITZALAN SQUARE 1902 48268

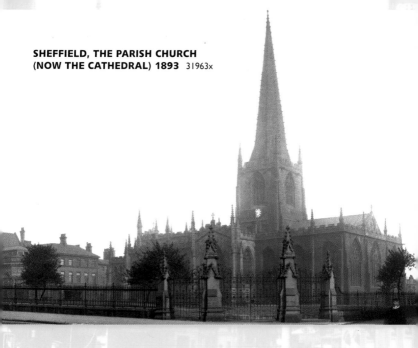

SHEFFIELD, THE PARISH CHURCH (NOW THE CATHEDRAL) 1893 31963x

Sheffield's original parish church of St Peter and St Paul was built in the 12th century, and rebuilt again in the late medieval period (see photograph 31963x, above). The church was granted cathedral status in 1914, and Dr Hedley Burrows was invested as the first Bishop of Sheffield and enthroned at the cathedral on 1 May 1914.

The word 'snig' in the name of Snig Hill in Sheffield probably refers to a block of wood that was used with cart wheels to act as a brake. As Snig Hill is on a steep slope that led to the town's manorial corn mill at Millsands, many a heavy load must have been braked on this steep hill in medieval times.

Sheffield's cathedral is famed for its Shrewsbury Chapel; among the monuments is one to George Talbot, the 6th Earl of Shrewsbury, who was burdened for many years with looking after Mary, Queen of Scots during her long period of captivity in England, from 1570 until 1584 (see photograph S108701, below). The Scottish queen was held captive for some time in Sheffield Castle, but was occasionally moved from the castle to Sheffield Manor Lodge.

SHEFFIELD, THE TOMB OF GEORGE TALBOT, 6TH EARL OF SHREWSBURY, THE CATHEDRAL 2005 S108701

Sheffield's cutlery industry was first recorded in 1297, when 'Robertus le coteler' – Robert the cutler – was listed as a taxpayer, and in 'The Reeve's Tale' of Chaucer's 'Canterbury Tales', written at the end of the 14th century, a character is mentioned carrying a 'Scheffeld thwitel', a pointed knife used for cutting and spearing food. In 1624, 498 master craftsmen in Sheffield and the surrounding villages were recorded: 440 knife makers, 31 shear and sickle makers, and 27 scissor makers. By the mid 17th century the industry was run by master craftsmen – 'little mesters' – doing business from small workshops attached to their cottages or at water-powered grinding wheels, where blades were forged, handles were fitted or 'hafted', and knives were finally assembled after the blades had been taken to a riverside cutlers' wheel to be ground on a grindstone. In the second half of the 20th century foreign competition in the cutlery industry was affecting Sheffield's trade, and Sheffield's once-great cutlery industry has now all but disappeared. Viner's of Sheffield, once the largest cutlery firm in the country, went out of business in 1982; its name and trademark were sold, and now appear on imported Korean cutlery.

Sheffield was recognised as a city in 1893, and plans were drawn up for the erection of a new Town Hall befitting one of the newest cities in the kingdom. Sheffield's gabled, Renaissance-style Town Hall, seen in photograph 37422 on page 47, was designed by E W Mountford and opened by Queen Victoria in 1897. Two friezes carved in stone on the exterior of the Town Hall reflect Sheffield's industrial history, depicting, among other things, grinders, smiths, smelters and miners. The Peace Gardens near the Town Hall were created on the site of the demolished St Paul's Church in 1938, and were so-named to commemorate the peace that was misguidedly expected from the Munich Agreement made by Britain's Prime Minister Neville Chamberlain with Nazi Germany that year. The gardens were redesigned in 1997-98 and now include water features and fountains.

**SHEFFIELD
A CEMENTATION FURNACE
DONCASTER STREET
2005** S108705

Until the second half of the 18th century the steel used by Sheffield's cutlers was either imported or was locally made 'shear steel' forged from 'blister steel' made in a cementation furnace. Some 260 such furnaces with their conical chimneys were eventually built in the Sheffield area, but photograph S108705 (opposite) shows the city's only remaining cementation furnace, on Doncaster Street. Crucible steel, which resulted in the growing international reputation of Sheffield as a steel-making centre, was developed by a local clock maker, Benjamin Huntsman, in the 1740s. He was dissatisfied with the quality of steel available to him for making clock springs so he experimented in producing a homogenous steel without variations in its carbon content. Crucible steel is so called because it was manufactured by putting broken bars of blister steel in small clay pots (crucibles) in a coke fire at very high temperatures for up to five hours. The end result was the ideal steel for cutlery and edge tool making, and by the 1850s around 90% of the country's crucible steel was made in Sheffield, as well as nearly 50% of all the steel made in Europe. The Bessemer process, invented by Henry Bessemer in the 1850s, revolutionised steel making in Sheffield in the 1860s. Using traditional methods of converting pig iron into blister steel and then into crucible steel took 14 or 15 days to produce a 40-50lb ingot of cast steel, whereas the Bessemer process could produce 6 tons of cast steel in about 30 minutes. The Bessemer converter made its first appearance in Sheffield on Carlisle Street at Bessemer's Steel Works in 1858. A Bessemer converter can now be seen at the Kelham Island Museum in Alma Street in Sheffield.

Old Sheffield Plate, as plated silver became known, was invented by a Sheffield cutler called Thomas Boulsover (1704-88), when he was repairing a knife handle made of silver and copper. He realised that a thin sheet of silver could be fused together with copper to give the impression of solid silver – and a new Sheffield trade was born. During the 18th century firms such as John Hoyland & Co, Joseph Hancock, and Tudor, Leader & Sherburn manufactured a wide range of plated silver articles such as snuff boxes, pocket flasks, buckles, buttons, candlesticks, as well as fancy 'holloware' such as coffee pots, jugs, dishes, bowls and trays.

Photograph 31961 (below) shows Fargate in Sheffield in the 1890s, at the heart of the city centre. The obelisk seen in this view was built to commemorate Queen Victoria's Jubilee of 1887; it was removed to Endcliffe Woods in 1903 and a statue of Queen Victoria replaced it here in 1905, but that was also taken to Endcliffe Woods in 1930.

SHEFFIELD, FARGATE AND SURREY STREET 1893 31961

SHEFFIELD, THE CANAL BASIN 1870 S108301

The Sheffield Canal, from the basin to Tinsley, was completed in 1819.
It joined the much older Don Navigation and from there went to the
Stainforth & Keaby Canal, offering Sheffield manufacturers a link with
the navigable River Trent and access to the ports of Hull and Grimsby.
In 1905 the New Junction Canal provided a link between the Don, the
Aire & Calder Navigation, and the port of Goole. Photograph S108301
(above) shows several barges at the busy Canal Basin in Sheffield in
the 1870s, loaded with scrap metal en route for reprocessing. The
Canal Basin is now Victoria Quays, and the Great Central Railway
sidings to the right of the photograph have disappeared.

**SHEFFIELD
THE CRIMEAN MONUMENT
1893** 31962

Photograph 31962 (opposite) shows the junction of South Street and Union Street in Sheffield, an area known as Moorhead, in the 1890s, with Sheffield's monument commemorating the Crimean War, complete with captured Russian cannons, in its original position – it was later moved to the Botanical Gardens.

Barker's Pool in Sheffield is so named because this is where a man called Barker made a pool in the 15th century for the storage of water, which was used to flush street filth and detritus all the way down to the Don. The pool was opened in the early hours of the morning. Barker's Pool was condemned as a public nuisance in 1793 and filled in. Photograph S108116 (below) shows Sheffield's War Memorial in Barker's Pool, unveiled in 1925. Sheffield formed a 'Pals' battalion in the First World War, the Sheffield City Battalion, which fought alongside the Accrington 'Pals' on 1 July 1916, the first day of the Somme offensive, to capture the village of Serre. Unfortunately the nature of the 'Pals' system meant that large numbers of men from one area who served and fought together would also die together, and the Sheffield City Battalion was almost annihilated – when the surviving members of the battalion were taken out of the line on 3 July, 513 officers and men had been killed or seriously wounded, or were missing in action.

SHEFFIELD, BARKER'S POOL
c1965 S108116

Many of Sheffield's traditional industries declined in the 1970s and early 1980s, including its famous heavy steel industry, but Sheffield has now turned the corner with a much more varied economy. The polluted, industrial Sheffield of the 18th century was described by Horace Walpole in 1760 as 'one of the foulest towns of England in the most charming situation', but 'Smoky Sheffield' is now a thing of the past, and the 21st-century city is an attractive place with a revitalised city centre. However, the creation of a new public plaza outside the city's railway station with water features and a 90m-long steel sculpture representing a knife blade, known as The Cutting Edge, will ensure that Sheffield's proud industrial heritage is never forgotten.

STOCKSBRIDGE, THE CLOCK TOWER c1960 S324016

BEAUCHIEF, THE ABBEY c1950 B335014

All that remains of the Premonstratensian abbey at Beauchief near Sheffield which was founded by Robert Fitz Ranulf around 1183 is the west tower, which dates from the 14th century (see photograph B335014, above). In the 1660s a small chapel dedicated to St Thomas Beckett was built against the east wall of the tower; many of its fittings including the pulpit, Communion table and box pews date from c1664.

Stocksbridge was formerly a busy steelmaking town in the valley of the Little Don River between Sheffield and Penistone. Stocksbridge has now been 'cleaned up' and no longer has the constant pall of smoke hanging over it that is seen in the background of photograph S324016 (opposite), taken around 1960, showing a view typical of many of the industrial towns of South Yorkshire in the past. The Clock Tower seen in this view was built in the 1920s as a war memorial.

HOYLAND, ELSECAR MAIN COLLIERY c1960 H218020

Hoyland, properly Hoyland Nether, is a large former coal mining
village between Sheffield and Barnsley. Elsecar Main Colliery, shown
in photograph H218020, above, was one of the many collieries which
formerly existed in the South Yorkshire coalfield around the village of
Hoyland. The winding wheels of two pitheads are visible in this view,
with a tall chimney of what was probably a coking plant in between.
The industrial heritage of the area is commemorated at the nearby
Elsecar Heritage Centre, located within the former ironworks and
colliery workshops.

The 'Miners' Welfare' was the community and cultural centre for many of South Yorkshire's coal mining villages, but not many were as grand as the one shown in photograph G110001 (below) at Goldthorpe, near Barnsley, built in 1923 with Tuscan-ordered entrance columns and elegant, classical proportions. Goldthorpe also has an unusual church, dedicated to St John the Evangelist and St Mary Magdalene. Constructed in 1916 in an Italian style designed by Arthur Nutt, it is an early example of a ferro-concrete building and is now Grade II listed.

GOLDTHORPE, THE MINERS' WELFARE HALL c1960 G110001

BARNSLEY, MARKET HILL 1948 B333004

Barnsley was founded by the monks of St John's Priory, Pontefract, after they had been granted the manor and rights to hold weekly markets and annual fairs. In the 18th and 19th centuries Barnsley was a centre of the linen industry, and many local people earned a living working with flax or bleaching and weaving linen. Another notable local industry was glassmaking, but Barnsley really developed in the 19th and 20th century as the centre of a major coalmining area – these two industries were of such importance to the town that a glassblower and a coal miner feature on the town's coat of arms.

Barnsley's Town Hall, with its monolithic central clock tower, was built of Portland stone in the early 1930s as a statement of civic pride (see photograph B333008, below). It stands high on the hill, looking regally down on the commercial heart of the town. The construction of the town hall was a sore point with the author George Orwell, who lived in Barnsley for a time whilst he was researching the lives of working-class coal miners for his book 'The Road to Wigan Pier'. He was very critical of the amount of money that the council spent on building the hall during the Great Depression, which he felt would have been better spent on improving the housing and living conditions for the working people of the town.

BARNSLEY, THE TOWN HALL c1950 B333008

Cawthorne near Barnsley was once the centre of a local iron and coal mining industry. In the scene shown in photograph C259023 (below) the lane past Fountain Cottage leads to the quiet surroundings of All Saints' Church. On the right of the photograph is the reconstructed 10th-century Anglian cross, put together from pieces dug up when the church was refurbished in the 1870s. Just outside Cawthorne is the 18th-century Cannon Hall, owned in the past by the Spencer-Stanhope family, and designed by John Carr of York. Sold to Barnsley Council in 1953, it is now a wonderful assemblage of stately home, formal gardens, a farm, and an ornamental lake. The house itself contains a fine collection of furniture, paintings, ceramics and glassware, as well as the Regimental Museum of the 13/18th Royal Hussars (Queen Mary's Own) and the Light Dragoons.

CAWTHORNE, MEMORIAL CORNER c1955 C259023

DONCASTER, STATION ROAD 1903 49854

King Richard I granted Doncaster a town charter in 1194, and in 1248 a charter was granted for a market to be held in the town. Doncaster thrived and prospered during the Middle Ages, and by 1334 it was the wealthiest town in southern Yorkshire, but the town owes its transformation from an agricultural to an industrial centre to the coming of the railways in the 19th century, when the Great Northern Railway chose Doncaster for the site of its locomotive and carriage and wagon workshops. The Doncaster Plant was particularly famous for building LNER 2, 4, and 6 Class locomotives such as the Mallard, the holder of the world speed record for steam locomotives, and the Flying Scotsman, notably used on the London to Edinburgh service, both of which are now in the National Railway Museum in York.

In the early part of the 20th century Doncaster became one of the largest coal mining areas in the country, and the town was ringed with pit villages. However, the local coal mining industry declined in the 1980s as elsewhere around the country, as pits were closed and most of the mining jobs were lost. In its heyday, Doncaster's coalfields helped to develop many other local industries, especially steel foundries, wire mills and glass production, many of which are still in business; Bridon (formerley British Ropes) is believed to be the largest wire rope manufacturing plant in Europe; and local firms such as Rockware Glass are still renowned high quality specialist glass manufacturers.

Photograph 49853 on page 51 shows Baxtergate in Doncaster. Many of the town's street names have 'gate' in their names. This derives from an old Scandinavian word for 'street' or 'the way to', and is a reminder of the time when much of Yorkshire was settled by people of Danish origin. In the Middle Ages, people plying the same craft or trade tended to live and work in the same part of town, and 'Baxtergate' originally meant 'the bakers' street'. The junction of Baxtergate, Frenchgate, St Sepulchre Gate and High Street is known as Clock Corner because of the huge clock on the tower that tops the building there, seen on the left of the photograph. There has been a clock on the site since 1731 but the present Clock Corner building was erected in 1894. In recent years the clock has been mended and restored. It plays a Westminster chime on the hour and every quarter from 8am to 10pm. In addition, for the ten days running up until Christmas the clock plays the Christmas carol 'Silent Night,' and on New Year's Eve it plays 'Auld Lang Syne'.

Photograph 31983 (below) shows the great parish church of St George at Doncaster, built in 1854-58 to a design by Sir George Gilbert Scott (and considered to be one of his finest works) to replace an earlier one which had been destroyed by fire some five years earlier. St George's Church was promoted to a minster in 2004.

DONCASTER, ST GEORGE'S CHURCH FROM THE SOUTH SIDE
1893 31983

DONCASTER, HIGH STREET 1895 35313

CONISBROUGH, THE CASTLE KEEP 1895 35320

Conisbrough Castle near Doncaster is one of the best-preserved Norman castles in the country. The tall, cylindrical keep, with its six massive semi-hexagonal buttresses which rise above it to form mini-turrets, was built about 1180 by Henry II's half-brother, Hamelin Plantagenet, and is thought to be the first of its type to be built in England; it was designed to be difficult to mine and resistant to attack with a battering ram (see photograph 35320, opposite). By the mid 16th century the castle was semi-derelict, and the fortress was in such poor condition that it was never garrisoned during the Civil War. It is believed that Hamelin Plantagenet might also have rebuilt Conisbrough's church, as much of the stonework is 12th-century. One of the most interesting features of the church is a carved Norman tomb-chest depicting various scenes including knights jousting, Adam and Eve, and a warrior fighting with a dragon.

The town of Askern is situated on the road between Doncaster and Selby, and from the 1820s it enjoyed brief fame as a spa; its strong sulphuretted medicinal waters were said to resemble those of Harrogate, and to be efficacious in the treatment of rheumatic and scorbutic disease, but were famously smelly. A certain Dr Chorley composed the following rhyme about the town:

> *'The devil when passing through Askron,*
> *Was asked what he thought thereon;*
> *Quoth Satan, Judging from the stink,*
> *I can't be far from home, I think'.*

The village of Sprotbrough near Doncaster was once famous for the welcome it offered to strangers. There used to be a cross in the village with a brass plate on it on which the following was inscribed: 'Whoso is hungry, and lists well to eat, Let him come to Sprotbrough, for his meat, And for a night and for a day, His horse shall have both corn and hay, And none shall ask him when he goes away'. The village was built around Sprotbrough Hall, but this was demolished in 1925, and only the name remains in street signs. The village's parish church dates mainly from the late 13th century, though the west tower is later; in 1474 William Fitzherbert left £40 in his will towards construction costs. In the chancel is an old stone seat, thought to be a sanctuary chair, and a brass of William Fitzherbert and his wife. Sir Walter Scott stayed in Sprotbrough whilst writing his novel 'Ivanhoe', hence the name of the Ivanhoe pub in Melton Road and a housing estate off Sprotbrough Road.

Thorne, near Doncaster, was once an important inland port linking the South Yorkshire coalfield and the River Don with the Aire & Calder Navigation and the River Humber via the Stainforth & Keadby Canal. It became a centre for the buying and selling of corn, coal and timber. From the top of the 13th-century tower of St Nicholas's parish church, six of the county's major rivers can be seen: the Humber, the Don, the Went, the Ouse, the Trent and the Aire. Flood defences were needed here, which were devised by the Dutch engineer Cornelius Vermuyden. In the late 19th century, many workers from Holland were attracted to this land of canals and windmills as skilled peat workers.

THORNE, MARKET PLACE c1955 T303029

NEW ROSSINGTON, KING AVENUE c1955 N73006

New Rossington, a village lying to the south of Doncaster, was created when the colliery was sunk into the rich South Yorkshire coalfield. It lies adjacent to the older village of Rossington, but took over in importance when mining became the local industry after coal reserves had been found here. The first pit was sunk in September 1912, and a 'New' Rossington was created for the colliers and their families. This small town was built in a radial pattern, and soon contained all the ingredients of urban life, including its own branch of the Doncaster Co-operative Society, seen on the right of photograph N73006, (above), which opened in 1915.

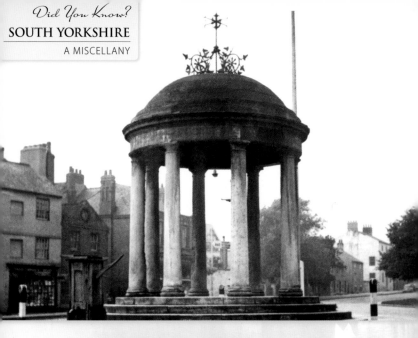

TICKHILL, THE CROSS c1960 T136012d

In medieval times Tickhill, which lies 4 miles south of Doncaster, was more important than Sheffield; its castle, built about 1130, was one of the most important in the north of England, built on a motte no less than 75ft high and surrounded by a moat 30ft wide. The original castle was built of wood, but it was replaced with stone in the early 12th century, probably by Henry I after he had confiscated the fortress from Robert de Belleme. The castle was held for King Charles I during the Civil War of the 17th century, and was razed in 1648 by order of Parliament to prevent its use as a stronghold in the future. The site of the castle is now a ruin with only the foundations of the keep remaining, together with some parts of the moat and courtyard walls, although the Norman gatehouse survives, built in 1129-1130.

The parish church of St Mary in Tickhill is considered to be one of the finest in Yorkshire, having been rebuilt in white magnesian limestone in the late 14th century, though some earlier parts still remain. Among the treasures are the tomb-chest of Thomas Fitzwilliam (died 1478), a late 15th-century font, and an early 17th-century pulpit. Photograph T136012d (opposite) shows the famous local landmark of the Buttercross in Tickhill's market place, which was erected in 1777 in an attempt to revive the town's weekly market.

The name of Rawmarsh near Rotherham is pronounced 'Romish' locally. Rawmarsh was known for its local potteries in the past, particularly for its earthenware, and this heritage is recalled in some of its street names, such as Claypit Lane and Pottery Lane. In more recent times, coal mining and the iron and steel industry were major employers in the Rawmarsh and Parkgate area. Rawmarsh's parish church of St Mary has origins in Norman times but the current church was mainly rebuilt in the 1830s and further work took place in 1869 on the tower, when features of a Norman doorway from a much earlier church on the site were incorporated. Inside the church are two interesting 17th-century monuments, one to Lady Middleton and her children (1667) who lived for a time at Aldwarke Hall, and the other to John Darley of Kilnhurst (1616).

Rotherham lies on the River Don, at its confluence with the River Rother. The settlement there began to develop as a market town near a ford over the River Don. In the 1480s Thomas Rotherham, Archbishop of York instigated the building of a theological college called The College of Jesus in Rotherham, where he was born in 1423; he is commemorated in the name of Thomas Rotherham College in the town. The College made Rotherham a famous centre of learning, but was dissolved by Henry VIII in 1547. The college occupied a site east of the parish church in the Effingham Street/College Street area; by 1583 the college had moved to premises elsewhere in the town, and the only surviving fragment of the medieval building is a doorway which was rebuilt into the face of an old quarry in Boston Park in Rotherham in 1876.

During the Middle Ages, travelling was such a dangerous business that many town bridges had chapels built on them so travellers could give thanks on reaching the town after a safe journey, or ask for a blessing before setting out. The Chapel of Our Lady standing on Rotherham Bridge dates from the 1480s, and is one of only four such medieval bridge chapels to survive in England (see photograph 36241, below). During the Civil War of the 17th century Rotherham Bridge was the scene of a spirited resistance by local people as they (unsuccessfully) defended the town against a Royalist force under the Earl of Newcastle, and gunshot holes can still be seen in the chapel walls. The chapel was used as the town gaol between 1775 and 1826, and graffiti carved by prisoners can be seen on the cell doors in the building.

ROTHERHAM, THE BRIDGE CHAPEL 1895 36241

ROTHERHAM, ALL SAINTS' CHURCH c1955 R60018

Rotherham Minster in Church Street is shown in photograph R60018 (left) when it was known as All Saints' Parish Church – it was granted minster status in 2004. One of the finest examples of Perpendicular architecture in Yorkshire, it was restored in 1873 by Sir George Gilbert Scott. The 180ft-high spire dominates the town. The minster is a Grade I listed building, and was described by Alec Clifton-Taylor in his list of England's best parish churches as 'the glory of Rotherham'. Other fans included Pevsner, who said it was 'the best perpendicular church in the country', and Simon Jenkins, who included it in 'England's 1000 Best Churches'. Inside the minster, the oak roof of the nave features 77 carved bosses, each of which is different from the others; also of interest are the medieval carved figurines on the bench ends in the chancel, known as 'poppy heads', which depict characters from the Annunciation and the Nativity.

The celebrated 19th-century author Anthony Trollope married his wife, a local girl called Rose Heseltine, in All Saints' Church in Rotherham (now Rotherham Minster) on 11th June 1844. Rose was the daughter of a Rotherham bank manager.

The Clifton Park Museum in Rotherham is renowned for its fine collection of Rockingham Pottery which was produced at Swinton, north of Rotherham, between 1745 and 1842. Internationally famous, the Rockingham Pottery manufactured fine porcelain in a finely decorated and rococo style. Some of the most famous items ever made by the Rockingham Pottery were the extravagantly and intricately decorated 'Rhinoceros Vases', created to showcase the work of the pottery and claimed to be the largest single-piece porcelain objects in the world. Only two 'Rhinoceros Vases' were made; one is in the Victoria and Albert Museum in London, and the other is in the Clifton Park Museum in Rotherham. Sadly, the Rockingham Pottery closed in 1842. One of the original kilns, a small part of the factory and the pottery flint mill pond survive at Swinton, where they can be found in a small park called Pottery Ponds off Blackamoor Road.

ROTHERHAM, THE TOWN HALL c1955 R60010

The Rotherham area was rich in coal seams, which were the impetus for improvements to the River Don and various cuttings to aid navigation and the transport of coal that resulted in the forming of the Sheffield and South Yorkshire Navigation. There were also abundant iron reserves in the area, and iron and steel making became the principal industry in Rotherham during the Industrial Revolution, a tradition which continued through the 19th century and lasted well into the 20th century. An important name amongst many others in the town's industrial heritage was that of the Walker family; in the 18th century the Walker foundries were renowned for producing high quality cannons, and Walker cannons were on board Lord Nelson's flagship the 'Victory' at the battle of Trafalgar in 1805, and used in the battle of Waterloo in 1815. This heritage is commemorated in present-day Rotherham, where three cannons feature on the town's coat of arms and an original Walker cannon stands in front of the Town Hall in Civic Square. The home of the Walker family was Clifton House in Clifton Park, which was designed by John Carr of York, one of the country's outstanding architects of his day. The 18th-century building is now the award-winning Clifton Park Museum.

The first glass works in Rotherham was established in 1751; as Beatson Clark & Co it became one of the town's largest manufacturers, exporting glass medicine bottles worldwide. The glass works is still operating on the same site, and still manufactures and sells glass containers for the pharmaceutical, food and drinks industries. A reminder of the area's early glassmaking heritage can be found at Catcliffe, near Rotherham, where William Fenney established a glassworks in 1740. One of his brick built glassmaking furnaces, the Catcliffe Glass Cone, still survives there; a Grade II listed building and a Scheduled Ancient Monument, it is the oldest example of a glass cone in western Europe.

Boston Park in Rotherham was formerly the property of the Earl of Effingham. In the grounds of the park is Boston Castle, which was built in the 1770s as a hunting lodge by the 3rd Earl of Effingham to mark his support for American colonists in their attempt to win independence from Britain. It was named after Boston in the USA, scene of 'The Boston Tea Party' of 1773 which was a key event in triggering the American War of Independence. Boston Park opened as the town's first public park in 1876 to celebrate the first centenary of the American Declaration of Independence.

Several streets in Rotherham are named after family connections of the 6th Earl of Effingham, a principle local landowner in the 19th century, who obtained a private Act of Parliament in 1851 to develop the town centre. These include Effingham Street, Howard Street and Frederick Street.

One of the oldest, most historic and best-loved buildings in Rotherham's town centre is the Imperial Buildings in Market Street. Built in 1907, this former Edwardian market building with a central covered glass quadrangle has now been restored and refurbished and houses apartments, cafes, bars and shops.

ROTHERHAM, THE TOWN CENTRE c1965 R60043

MALTBY, ROCHE ABBEY 1893 31978

Despite being an ancient settlement, Maltby near Rotherham was still
little more than a village at the beginning of the 20th century. Then
in 1902 the Sheepbridge Coal & Iron Co leased land from the Earl of
Scarbrough, and in 1906 the Maltby Main Colliery Co was formed. At
its height the colliery employed several thousand miners, and Maltby's
population rose to over 15,000. Near Maltby are the ruins of Roche
Abbey, founded in 1147 as a colony of Newminster in Northumberland,
itself a daughter house of the great Cistercian abbey of Fountains in
Yorkshire. The abbey took its name from a cross-like rock that was
already an object of pilgrimage for the faithful. In 1538 Roche Abbey
was surrendered to the Crown as part of Henry VIII's Dissolution and
destroyed. The choir stalls were fired to melt lead; timber and stone
were sold off as the great building was reduced to little more than a
quarry. The main ruins we see today comprise part of the east walls of
the transepts, part of the chancel and a vaulted gatehouse.

SHEFFIELD, ENDCLIFFE WOODS 1893 31976

SPORTING SOUTH YORKSHIRE

There have been race meetings in Doncaster since 1600, but it was the St Leger of 1776 that put the town on the racing calendar. The race was named after a neighbour of Lord Rockingham, Lt Gen Anthony St Leger. Rockingham commissioned the building of the grandstand in 1778; it was a copy of John Carr's original stand at the York Knavesmire course. A new grandstand opened in 1970.

A famous sports personality from Thorne near Doncaster is Gillian Coultard (born 1963), who captained the England women's football team in the 1990s, and was capped over 120 times for representing her country. She also has a place in footballing history as the first woman to have scored a goal at Wembley stadium.

Sheffield is fortunate to have a number of top class sporting arenas, including Bramall Lane, Hillsborough and the Don Valley Stadium. The Don Valley Stadium built to be ready for the World Student Games in 1991. It remains Britain's biggest athletics stadium with some of the best facilities, including the country's strongest floodlights. Bramall Lane, home of Sheffield United Football Club, is thought to be the oldest major ground which still hosts professional football matches. It also has the distinction of being one of only two grounds to have staged an England cricket match against Australia, an England football international, and an FA Cup final. The Oval in London is the other.

Sheffield can claim to be the home of the world's two oldest football clubs. Sheffield FC was founded in 1857 and is officially recognised as the world's oldest club now playing association football. Hallam FC was founded just three years later and is also still in existence, playing its matches at its original ground, Sandygate. Hallam FC took part in what was probably the first football tournament under the modern rules, the Youdan Cup, held in the city in 1867. Hallam FC won the final, which was played at Bramall Lane.

The name of Sheffield Wednesday Football Club was originally 'the Wednesday Cricket Club'. A cricket team of that name was established in the early 19th century and later a football team was set up in association with it. For many years the football club was known as 'The Wednesday', before its official name was changed to Sheffield Wednesday FC in the late 1920s.

The Crucible Theatre in Sheffield, opened in 1871, has gained the city national and international importance – but not for theatrical importance on its thrust stage or in its studio theatre. It is best known as the venue for the annual World Snooker Championships.

The nickname of Rotherham United Football Club is 'The Millers', reflecting the importance of grain milling in the town in the past, especially in the Millmoor area. A famous footballer from Rotherham was David Seaman, born in the town in 1963, who went on to great success as a goalkeeper playing for Arsenal; he also played 75 times for England, making him the national team's most capped goalkeeper after Peter Shilton.

Barnsley Football Club, nicknamed 'The Tykes', was founded in 1887 as Barnsley St Peter's. Barnsley FC won the FA Cup in 1912, but the 2007-08 FA Cup tournament was also notable for a terrific run for The Tykes, when Barnsley reached the semi-final having defeated Liverpool (2-1) and Chelsea (1-0), before going out to Cardiff City. In the 2008/09 season, Barnsley Football Club fielded the youngest ever player in the history of the Football League at Ipswich Town when Reuben Noble-Lazarus came on aged 15 years and 45 days, beating the record previously held by Albert Geldard of Bradford (Park Avenue) FC.

Rugby players are known for their macho image, but Barnsley Rugby League Club (now known as Barnsley Broncos Rugby League Club) proudly turned out for every match of the 2009 season wearing bright pink kits to show their support for Yorkshire Cancer Research.

The village of Cudworth on the outskirts of Barnsley has an impressive record of producing famous sportspeople, including Archibald Stinchcombe, who won an Olympic gold medal in 1936 with the British ice-hockey team, and David Hirst, the former Barnsley FC, Sheffield Wednesday FC and England footballer. But the most famous sporting personality from Cudworth is the athlete Dorothy Hyman, born there in 1941, after whom the Dorothy Hyman Stadium is named, home of Barnsley Athletics Club. Dorothy Hyman was one of Britain's most successful sprinters. She won a silver medal in the 100 metres at the 1960 Olympics and a bronze in the 200 metres, and was part of the GB 4 x 100 metres relay team which won a bronze medal in the 1964 Olympics. She also won a gold medal in the 100 metres and a silver in the 200 metres at the 1962 European Championships, and won both the 100 metres and 200 metres at the 1962 Commonwealth Games. She was voted BBC Sports Personality of the Year in 1963.

QUIZ QUESTIONS

Answers on page 52.

1. Who are known respectively as 'The Bard of Barnsley' and 'The Barnsley Nightingale'?

2. What is the link between a South Yorkshire village and the American custom of Thanksgiving, observed in the United States on the 4th Thursday in November each year?

3. The inventor of the flushing toilet was a South Yorkshire man. Who was he, and where was he born?

4. What sport is played by the Sheffield Steelers?

5. What did the term 'rattening' refer to in Sheffield in the past?

6. Sheffield's magnificent Town Hall is shown in photograph 37422, opposite. The tower of the Town Hall is 210ft high, and topped off with a bronze statue by Mario Raggi of Vulcan, who has been associated with the city for many years, and appears as a supporter on Sheffield's coat of arms – but who was Vulcan?

7. Where in South Yorkshire can you find a house with the covetable address of 'Number One Yorkshire'?

8. What is the origin of the name of Doncaster?

9. Rotherham Minster is famous for an unusually large number of … what?

10. Which South Yorkshire company invented an essential household item used in kitchens and bathrooms?

SHEFFIELD, THE TOWN HALL 1896 37422

RECIPE

BARNSLEY CHOPS WITH PORT AND REDCURRANT SAUCE

A special cut for a lamb chop is named after the South Yorkshire town of Barnsley – a Barnsley chop is cut from the centre of the loin across both chops, producing a butterfly shape. The Barnsley chop is believed to have originated from the Brooklands Hotel in the town. In this recipe, the sauce made with redcurrant jelly accompanies the rich flavour of lamb beautifully. If Barnsley chops prove hard to find, lamb loin chops can be used instead.

> Allow 1 Barnsley lamb chop per person
> A little oil for brushing the chops
> Salt and pepper to taste
> 4 tablespoonfuls of redcurrant jelly
> 1 wine glass of port

Melt the redcurrant jelly in a small saucepan, then add the port and bring to the boil. Allow to boil for five minutes to reduce down, then turn the heat to low and keep the sauce warm whilst you cook the chops.

Season the chops with salt and pepper, then either fry in a little oil or brush them with a little oil and place them under a pre-heated grill and cook for about 8-10 minutes, or less if you like your lamb very pink, turning the chops over half way through the cooking time. They should be well browned on the outside, but slightly pink in the middle.

Serve the chops piping hot, accompanied with the sauce.

BARNSLEY, SHEFFIELD ROAD c1950 B333001

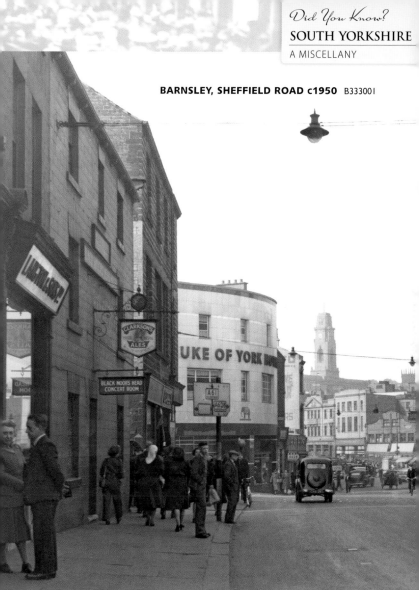

RECIPE

APPLE FRITTERS

Apple fritters used to be a traditional treat in many parts of Yorkshire for Ash Wednesday, the first day of Lent and 46 days before Easter in the Christian religious calendar.

> 225g/8oz flour
> 3 eggs
> 300ml/ ½ pint of milk
> 225g/8oz currants
> 4 cooking apples
> Lard or oil for frying
> Caster or icing sugar for dredging

Sift the flour into a large mixing bowl and make a well in the centre. Break the eggs into the well, and beat them into the flour, drawing the flour in from the sides, until it has all mixed together thoroughly into a smooth paste. Gradually add the milk, a little at a time, beating continually to make a batter.

Peel and core the apples and chop them into small pieces. Mix the apple pieces and the currants into the batter.

Heat the lard or oil in a large pan. Drop in spoonfuls of the batter and fry the fritters until they are crisp and golden. Drain and dry on absorbent kitchen paper, then dredge with sugar and eat whilst still hot.

DONCASTER, BAXTERGATE 1903 49853

QUIZ ANSWERS

1. 'The Barnsley Bard' is Ian McMillan, born in Darfield in Barnsley in 1956, who is a well-known poet, journalist, playwright and broadcaster. He writes a weekly column in The Barnsley Chronicle, and is also poet in residence to Barnsley Football Club. 'The Barnsley Nightingale' is the English folk singer and songwriter Kate Rusby, born in Sheffield in 1973 but now a resident of Penistone, in the Metropolitan Borough of Barnsley. She was described by The Guardian newspaper as 'a superstar of the British acoustic scene', and in 2006 her beautiful voice came to a wider audience when she dueted with Ronan Keating on the hit song 'All Over Again'.

2. The village of Austerfield near Doncaster was the birthplace in 1590 of William Bradford, one of the Pilgrim Fathers who sailed for America on board the 'Mayflower' in 1620, and went on to become the Governor of Plymouth Colony in Massachusetts. William Bradford is credited as the instigator of the American Thanksgiving celebration, when in 1621 the Plymouth colonists and Wampanoag Native Americans shared an autumn harvest feast to give thanks for a successful bounty of crops.

3. The inventor of the flushing toilet was Thomas Crapper, who was born at Thorne near Doncaster in 1837.

4. The Sheffield Steelers is the name of Sheffield's ice-hockey team.

5. 'Rattening' was a term used in Sheffield in the second half of the 19th century for the confiscation by trade unionists of a workman's tools on behalf of trade societies, to persuade workers to join a union or to make them stop working for masters paying less than the recommended rate.

6. Vulcan was the Roman god of fire and furnaces, and thus most appropriate for Sheffield. The statue on top of Sheffield's Town Hall depicts a large nude figure holding a hammer in his right hand and arrows in his left, with his right foot resting on an anvil.

7. At Bawtry, near Doncaster. Bawtry was once a coaching stop on the old Great North Road, where horses were changed on the journey north to Scotland. It had also been an important port on the River Idle since Roman times, linking to the Humber. Bawtry is situated on the county boundary with Nottinghamshire, and for this reason is often called 'the Gateway to Yorkshire' – and the southernmost house on entering the town on the Great North Road off the A638 from Nottinghamshire carries the covetable address of 'Number One Yorkshire'.

8. During the Roman period, a fort was built at Doncaster to guard a crossing place across the River Don. The name of the fort was first recorded as 'Caer Daun', but it was later known as 'Danum', which gave Doncaster the first part of its name; the 'caster' part derives from an Anglo-Saxon corruption of the Latin word 'Castra' for a military camp. The site of the Roman fort is believed to have been where the minster church of St George now stands.

9. Rotherham Minster is renowned for the faces of over 30 'Green Men' which can be found hidden amidst the carved foliage that decorates the pillars of the nave. Although it probably derived from a pagan symbol, perhaps symbolising a fertility figure or a nature spirit, a carving of a Green Man is commonly found in medieval churches and is believed to have been used as a symbol of spring, or rebirth; however, it is most unusual to find as many examples of Green Men in one church as there are in Rotherham Minster.

10. The Rotherham brass founders Guest and Chrimes are credited with inventing the household tap – the company patented and manufactured the first screw-down tap mechanism in 1845.

FRANCIS FRITH

PIONEER VICTORIAN PHOTOGRAPHER

Francis Frith, founder of the world-famous photographic archive, was a complex and multi-talented man. A devout Quaker and a highly successful Victorian businessman, he was philosophical by nature and pioneering in outlook. By 1855 he had already established a wholesale grocery business in Liverpool, and sold it for the astonishing sum of £200,000, which is the equivalent today of over £15,000,000. Now in his thirties, and captivated by the new science of photography, Frith set out on a series of pioneering journeys up the Nile and to the Near East.

INTRIGUE AND EXPLORATION

He was the first photographer to venture beyond the sixth cataract of the Nile. Africa was still the mysterious 'Dark Continent', and Stanley and Livingstone's historic meeting was a decade into the future. The conditions for picture taking confound belief. He laboured for hours in his wicker dark-room in the sweltering heat of the desert, while the volatile chemicals fizzed dangerously in their trays. Back in London he exhibited his photographs and was 'rapturously cheered' by members of the Royal Society. His reputation as a photographer was made overnight.

VENTURE OF A LIFE-TIME

By the 1870s the railways had threaded their way across the country, and Bank Holidays and half-day Saturdays had been made obligatory by Act of Parliament. All of a sudden the working man and his family were able to enjoy days out, take holidays, and see a little more of the world.

With typical business acumen, Francis Frith foresaw that these new tourists would enjoy having souvenirs to commemorate their days out. For the next thirty years he travelled the country by train and by pony and trap, producing fine photographs of seaside resorts and beauty spots that were keenly bought by millions of Victorians. These prints were painstakingly pasted into family albums and pored over during the dark nights of winter, rekindling precious memories of summer excursions. Frith's studio was soon supplying retail shops all over the country, and by 1890 F Frith & Co had become the greatest specialist photographic publishing company in the world, with over 2,000 sales outlets, and pioneered the picture postcard.

FRANCIS FRITH'S LEGACY

Francis Frith had died in 1898 at his villa in Cannes, his great project still growing. By 1970 the archive he created contained over a third of a million pictures showing 7,000 British towns and villages.

Frith's legacy to us today is of immense significance and value, for the magnificent archive of evocative photographs he created provides a unique record of change in the cities, towns and villages throughout Britain over a century and more. Frith and his fellow studio photographers revisited locations many times down the years to update their views, compiling for us an enthralling and colourful pageant of British life and character.

We are fortunate that Frith was dedicated to recording the minutiae of everyday life. For it is this sheer wealth of visual data, the painstaking chronicle of changes in dress, transport, street layouts, buildings, housing and landscape that captivates us so much today, offering us a powerful link with the past and with the lives of our ancestors.

Computers have now made it possible for Frith's many thousands of images to be accessed almost instantly. The archive offers every one of us an opportunity to examine the places where we and our families have lived and worked down the years. Its images, depicting our shared past, are now bringing pleasure and enlightenment to millions around the world a century and more after his death.

For further information visit: www.francisfrith.com

INTERIOR DECORATION

Frith's photographs can be seen framed and as giant wall murals in thousands of pubs, restaurants, hotels, banks, retail stores and other public buildings throughout Britain. These provide interesting and attractive décor, generating strong local interest and acting as a powerful reminder of gentler days in our increasingly busy and frenetic world.

FRITH PRODUCTS

All Frith photographs are available as prints and posters in a variety of different sizes and styles. In the UK we also offer a range of other gift and stationery products illustrated with Frith photographs, although many of these are not available for delivery outside the UK – see our web site for more information on the products available for delivery in your country.

THE INTERNET

Over 100,000 photographs of Britain can be viewed and purchased on the Frith web site. The web site also includes memories and reminiscences contributed by our customers, who have personal knowledge of localities and of the people and properties depicted in Frith photographs. If you wish to learn more about a specific town or village you may find these reminiscences fascinating to browse. Why not add your own comments if you think they would be of interest to others? See **www.francisfrith.com**

PLEASE HELP US BRING FRITH'S PHOTOGRAPHS TO LIFE

Our authors do their best to recount the history of the places they write about. They give insights into how particular towns and villages developed, they describe the architecture of streets and buildings, and they discuss the lives of famous people who lived there. But however knowledgeable our authors are, the story they tell is necessarily incomplete.

Frith's photographs are so much more than plain historical documents. They are living proofs of the flow of human life down the generations. They show real people at real moments in history; and each of those people is the son or daughter of someone, the brother or sister, aunt or uncle, grandfather or grandmother of someone else. All of them lived, worked and played in the streets depicted in Frith's photographs.

We would be grateful if you would give us your insights into the places shown in our photographs: the streets and buildings, the shops, businesses and industries. Post your memories of life in those streets on the Frith website: what it was like growing up there, who ran the local shop and what shopping was like years ago; if your workplace is shown tell us about your working day and what the building is used for now. Read other visitors' memories and reconnect with your shared local history and heritage. With your help more and more Frith photographs can be brought to life, and vital memories preserved for posterity, and for the benefit of historians in the future.

Wherever possible, we will try to include some of your comments in future editions of our books. Moreover, if you spot errors in dates, titles or other facts, please let us know, because our archive records are not always completely accurate—they rely on 140 years of human endeavour and hand-compiled records. You can email us using the contact form on the website.

Thank you!

For further information, trade, or author enquiries please contact us at the address below:

The Francis Frith Collection, Oakley Business Park, Wylye Road, Dinton, Wiltshire SP3 5EU.
Tel: +44 (0)1722 716 376 Fax: +44 (0)1722 716 881
e-mail: sales@francisfrith.co.uk **www.francisfrith.com**